VOICES IN
GIANT CITIES

ALSO BY R. CLIFT

TO FEEL ANYTHING AT ALL
TO BE REMEMBERED
TOMORROW WILL BE KINDER

UNTIL WE MEET AGAIN
YOUR THOUGHTS DESERVE A DECENT PLACE TO LIVE
THE POETRY OF WILDFLOWERS: FIELD JOURNAL
BEAUTY EXISTS SO CLOSE TO AGONY

UNSENT LOVE LETTERS: AN ANTHOLOGY OF WORDS LEFT UNSPOKEN
THE ART & POETRY OF TRAVELERS: VOL I

VOICES IN GIANT CITIES

a collection of poetry

by

R. Clift

THE CONSTELLATION POET

NYC · LA · PAR · ROM · EDI · LDN
2021 | 2022 | 2023

COPYRIGHT 2024 BY R. CLIFT.
All rights reserved.
First printing edition, 2024.

ISBN: 978-1-960045-03-4.

COVER DESIGN BY R. CLIFT.
COVER ELEMENTS BY EDWARD HOPPER
AND ABBOTT HANDERSON THAYER.

AUTHOR PHOTO BY LAURA CLIFT.

*To the strangers who inspired this book
and will never read it*

Introduction

Most of my life, I have been wary of giant cities. Growing up at the edge of nowhere— not much was more foreign to me than the idea of being thrown into hoards of people when walking out the front door. The constant sounds, the maze of streets, the overwhelming stimulation.

In years past, I've visited each of these cities several times, and back then, I thought— eventually— something would click and I would settle in. I would feel innate. But it never happened.

In 2021, as the world began to open up, I wished to travel again. To explore, to be around people, to visit old friends, to reconnect with these cities like they— in some way— were old friends too.

My initial inspiration for this collection came from reading a book called *Voices in a Giant City* published in 1947. I first discovered it in Edinburgh in 2018 (see pg. 97). The author, A.S.J. Tessimond, quickly became one of my favorite poets. Many of my poems mirror his directly— this was very much done on purpose. If he could have his finger on the pulse of one city, then surely I could find the heartbeat of another.

Writing this collection while traveling was my way of searching for the beauty in chaos. Of looking closer instead of turning away. I figured, if I could break down these overwhelming cities into small moments, single heartbeats that made me feel intrinsic, then maybe I could find a way to love— or at least better understand— the whole.

This is a book of voices. Voices of strangers, friends, buildings and bus stops, icons and hidden corners no one would normally look twice at. Through the years, my guiding notion was to write about what inspired me enough to stop me in my tracks, even if it was unexpected. This was not necessarily the most famous attraction in town, but quite often the overlooked.

My hope was to find some sense of belonging. To reach out and claim moments as my own in each city, to allow them, in return, to claim pieces of me— of my memories.

I carried the same little green notebook through all of my travels, writing every poem in this collection first by hand. Once I filled it up— I knew it was time to share them here with you.

Each poem is paired with latitude & longitude coordinates at the bottom of the page— if you look these up, you will see where I actually was when the poem was being written. If desired, it may offer more insight into my verses, and maybe— when you find yourself traveling through one of these cities, you may visit some of these places, and see them the way a poet once did.

Rachel Clift
November, 2023

Contents

PAGE

New York City
THE TAXI DRIVER	3
THE COMMUTERS	4
GHOSTS IN THE MUSEUM	6
THE MOMENT BEFORE I FALL	7
THE DEAD POET	8
TO A GIRL WHO WOULD LIKE TO STAY	9
GALLERY 548	10
SONDER	12
WOLLMAN RINK	13
THE STONEWALL INN	14
NIGHT OF JOY	15
C TRAIN: LAST STOP EUCLID AV	17
WILLIAMSBURG CAFE, 2023	18
THE HIGH LINE	19
SKYLINE	20

Los Angeles
ROSEWOOD AVE	25
HOLLYWOOD	26
THE PACIFIC	28
SANTA MONICA PIER	29
THE ONES YOU LEAVE BEHIND	30
I-FIVE NORTH	32
LOCALS ONLY	33
THE MUSICIAN	34
VIDE NOIR	36
THE COFFEE SHOP	37
THE HIDDEN ARTISTS	38
EROS	40
LUMIÈRE CINÉMATOGRAPHE	42
LAX	43
THE ABBEY	45
A CAGED BIRD SET FREE	46
BOATS AGAINST THE CURRENT	48

	PAGE
Paris	
The Only Stars Visible in the City of Light	53
La Dame de Fer	55
Les Échos du Passé	56
The Poet of Notre Dame	57
La Nuit Étoilée, 1888	58
À Vous de Jouer, Gare de l'Est	59
Thunderstorms in Tuileries Garden	60
The Watercolorist	62
L'Île aux Oiseaux	63
59 Rue de Rivoli	64
Renaissance Boy	65
Temple de l'Amour	66
Midsummer Muses	68
Jardin Tino Rossi	69
Lovers on the Terrace	70
Let them live Quietly	71
Le Jardin de Sacré Couer	73
Wall of Love	74
Artist 64	75
Always & Always	76
Rome	
Coins in a Fountain	81
The Harpist	82
Terrazza Viale del Belvedere	83
The Rambling Man	84
The Nameless Woman	85
Roman Cafe, 2022	86
Stargazers	87
Galileo	88
Tavolo 40	89
Leaving the Past Behind	90
Edinburgh	
Princes Street Gardens	95
The Old Man of the Blue Bookshop	97
Royal Mile	98
Edinburgh Cafe, 2022	99
The Professor	100
The Seabirds	102
Horoscope for Diana	103

	PAGE
THE LOVERS	104
THE ADDICTS	105
THE LOTHIANS	106
ROSEBURN TERRACE	107

London

ST. DUNSTAN-IN-THE-EAST	113
SONG OF TRAFALGAR SQUARE	114
THE IMPRESSIONISTS, ROOM 44	115
KYOTO GARDEN	116
PADDINGTON	117
HOPE SPEAKS TO THE HESITANT	119
SONG IN COVENT GARDEN	120
THE PERFECT STRANGER	121
THE GLOUCESTER ARMS	122
OLD FLAME	123
THE ACTOR	124
POETS' CORNER	125
EAST-FACING WINDOW	127
HOLLAND PARK	128
ANOTHER ENGLISH PUB	130
CRUEL TO BE KIND	131
THE ENCHANTED BOOKSTORE	132
ARTISTS ADMIRING ARTISTS	133
GRAVE OF THE UNKNOWN WARRIOR	135
SUMMER PARK PATHWAY, 2023	136
HEAVEN'S GATE	138
KEEP THE SECRET LOCKED IN YOUR HEART	139
LOVE FROM KEW	140
INNOCENCE & SADNESS	141

Other Cities

THE FLOATING CITY	146
THE CITY OF FOG	147
THE SECRET LIBRARY	149
THE DOCENT	150
SKELETON CREW	151
A CONVERSATION FOR THREE	152
THE CITY OF LILIES	153
EPILOGUE	155
DEDICATIONS	159
ABOUT THE AUTHOR	157

> "The words 'I am...' are potent words; be careful what you hitch them to. The thing you're claiming has a way of reaching back and claiming you."
>
> – A.L. KITSELMAN

New York City

AUTUMN 2022
WINTER 2023

The Taxi Driver

I AM the one you look at— you look
through— only ever from behind.
The darkened back of a head—
never to look in the eye. I am
the ferryman, two pennies to go
wherever you need to be— it doesn't
matter to me— as long as
        I am paid.

For so long, I have been traversing
this maze of endless streets, this
grid-lock labyrinth— without
even trying to escape— I am
the comfort of knowing what's
around the corner— what's around
        every corner.

You will not know my name,
the shape of my face when
I laugh or cry— but it is me
you turn to in the middle
of the night and you know I
will be there, every time, with
a different face— an altered soul,
but you'd never be able
        to tell the difference.

40.7580° N
73.9855° W

The Commuters

We are the worker bees,
the placid ones, the
nation's backbone on
      the verge of breaking—
too spineless to claw our
way out of the jungle—
too comfortable to even
attempt to leave, like
laying on a bed of nails
      from cradle to grave,
terrified of one wrong move
taking all we've worked for
away, never daring to
venture from the assurance
of a set schedule made
by someone else with
      an illusion of authority.
We walk too quickly
to get to places we don't
      want to go—
we laugh too little and sigh
too loud— we leave early
because we have to get to
work in the morning and
we never fight back because
payday is next week and
we're saving up for something
we don't need.

But it's not just us at
        fault, you see, not entirely—
we've been told all our lives
this is what happiness looks
like. We numb ourselves with
material things, tv screens, and
        pretty lies— for the only way
to cope with this existence is
to trudge through each day half-alive.

40.7534° N
73.9768° W

Ghosts in the Museum

MANHATTAN is quiet tonight
and everything that understood you
      is five years away.
I am the whispers of days
      long past and memories
faded to nothing but photographs
and flashbulb conversations. I am
standing in the same place and
never feeling the same. I am who
you used to be and who she
longed to become. I am every
version in between and the next
      you have yet to meet. I am
trillions of years of stories told
and the one that hurts
the most just happens to be your
      own.

The Moment Before I Fall

MIDTOWN— why do I shiver
at the thought of being
    lost in your alleys?
I am but a tender autumn
leaf, swept away from its
home tree— out of the
forest and into the
chaos— I am untethered,
unbound, yet afraid
to touch the ground.
What if I get lost,
    or hurt, or taken?
What if I was never
supposed to leave the safety
of canopy— what if—
no matter how hard I try—
I will always be horrified
    by a city this giant?

40.7740° N
73.9710° W

The Dead Poet

I am a hole-in-the-wall at the
west edge of the world. Foxed
pages and crumbling spines—
brick walls sheltering books
filled with hidden messages.
      A low hum resonates
to lull you to another
world— past love, labor,
      and loss—
      to one where
your thoughts are gentle
and you can feel your heart
beating in your
      own chest—
      you can feel
the wind swirl past your
fingertips and for once
it doesn't only remind you
of the empty space in
between.

40.7850° N
73.9773° W

To a Girl who would Like to Stay

She is tied to this place—
her pulse beating
            in sync with
the pounding of footsteps on
pavement, veins
like underground
train tracks— transporting, carrying,
moving— blood pumping,
        never
sleeping, never stopping, never
            ceasing,
to give in is to resign herself
to living a lie—
half-alive, torn
from the city
that mirrors her own
soul— restless, stubborn,
        desperate
                to belong.

Gallery 548

I AM a stone-cold tangle of
rooms filled with treasures
old and new— I am the
mysterious Renoir eyes
calling to your curiosity
from across the room—

I am the color faded
from Van Gogh's blooms—
I am the silent walls
built to surround you
in Degas and Monet
and Pisarro. When you
ask to be known in
these halls I answer
in marble— Rodin
around every corner—
the hand of god, the
gates of hell, the martyr
falling from her pedestal—

in the curve of her
jaw you may find the
answers you seek— but
if you look even closer
you will see the grief of
an artist who was too
afraid to look another

in the eye and admit
he was breaking—
and just before
      you walk away—

you will notice
all that's left
in the etching
of his name is
an echo of bravery
and a drop of pain
      still bleeding out
like the letters
are nothing but scars
that never had
      the chance to heal.

Sonder

We are incandescent stars trapped
in glass boxes stacked up on
one another to build a highrise
tall enough to scrape against
the stratosphere. We are
strangers behind every closed
door and every pair of headlights
flying by— we are millions
captivating stories you will
never read— we are the life
and breath of this city—
we are droplets in
              a raging sea—
you will never know what
it is like to be so
engrained— to be
such a part of a place
it is as if you are the
very blood in its veins.
              As if you,
and only you,
can keep it alive.

Wollman Rink

I WILL give you silver wings
and a hand to hold—

I will test your will
to fly, be brave,
be fast, be cold—

serendipity on your
tongue and determination
in your eye— around
and around you will
soar, never to go any
further than just
beyond your reach
of reality,
        catching
a glimpse of one
where you may
become as
        magnificent
as the sky.

The Stonewall Inn

Love is love is love
is love and I will
hold you safely in the
palm of my hand.

I will fashion a shield
from the hearts of
those who have
lived and died for
the right to be, listen
to these speakers
roar, feel the music
move through your
body and know that
here, you may dance
with whomever you wish.
May the world, one day,
be as welcoming.

Night of Joy
Written with Em

Flowers trapped in tile— won't you stay
      for a while?
I will hold your laughter and conversation,
neon fading, amber bulbs illuminating
      old friends
           and new faces.
Gentle chaos surrounding and sparks of
wannabe lovers as warming as the cocktail
burning down her throat.
      Candles in the fireplace,
brocade curtains, ornate frames—
sailboats engraved, stained paper
FIND YOUR DIRECTION
WHILE LOSING YOUR
PATH, EACH SEAT
      IS FOR PAY...

LEAVE WITH YOU
A SENSE OF BELONGING—
TRY YOUR HAND AT
      THE HAPPENING—

UNTIL YOU LAND AT
      judgement day.

OBSERVATIONS
WRITTEN BY VMW

Sizzling grill, clanking
of plates & silverware;
laughter & giggles that
are easily recognizable
through foreign languages.

A familiar & new soundtrack.
Two voices that I've known
for years; in this lifetime &
 the last.

C Train: Last Stop Euclid Av

Two muses guide me
      through—
easy to follow,
effortless to trust,
always leading me
back to an innate
      sense of safety.
Inspired by the stars
and pushed by the
universe— in a swirl of
souls I will never know—
a handful are held closer
      than all the rest,
and in the small presence
of only those— and the
years we have known—

sitting between the two of you
is where I feel
      most at home.

Williamsburg Cafe, 2023

I AM ivory keys echoing
through tall ceilings, pens
scratching on borrowed
                paper—
aching to capture
a moment, a memory,
a feeling of belonging—
of family— of peace.

There are quiet moments,
like this eye of the storm,
that can only be found
and felt as they are in a city
of eight and a half million
                beating hearts.
Do not mistake
this quietness for
emptiness— for this is
as necessary as the air
that surrounds you and
                fills your lungs.
So, when you come across
a moment of stillness like this—
do not take it for granted.

            Breathe it in.

The High Line

WILDFLOWERS growing through the
tracks, nature taking back
what was once a place
hardly ever able to be walked,
touched, appreciated—
         and now—
rudbeckia bloom alongside
skyscrapers and winding
walkways lead you closer
to the orange horizon.
Honeybees buzz like yellow
taxis below flying down
avenues and boulevards— people
look up from their distractions
and smile at each other—
strangers striking up conversations
like old friends— and when you find
yourself in this impossible space
caught between wild and
         concrete—
you realize nothing in this world
is ever quite as it seems.
Nothing in this world ever
has to stay the same—
and above all— it is
never too late
         to change.

40.7178° N
73.9544° W

Skyline

Headlights on the highway
and glowing windows dot
every high rise—
each light
obscuring a life
I will never
        know.
As an observer,
I cannot help
but stare—
though there
is not much
        more
to see than flowers
in the window
and shadows
behind soft
white curtains.

What is it like—
being surrounded
by so many lives
you'll never
be a part of?
Does it make you
        feel less
or more
alone?

40.7029° N
73.9967° W

Los Angeles

SUMMER 2021
SPRING 2022
AUTUMN 2022

Rosewood Ave

I am the violinist behind
a single-lit window—
    solemn notes making
their way through darkened
    streets.
I am unexpected, like a
voice that calls your name
    through silence,
stopping you in
    your tracks—
sheltering you from the
rush of your own
mind— begging you
to stop and consider
this fleeting moment
as significant. A transient
melody cascades over
you until your impatience
drowns it out— you turn
and walk away—
fading into the night,
leaving the violin behind—
    singing only to
        the stars.

Hollywood

Where the breeze
      carries ambition
across rolling hills—
deep into the valley.

Where dreams settle
and burrow down
      into the earth.

Where stars burn
themselves to dust
because the limelight
      is all that matters.

I am the lost generation,
whispers through the ages
of hidden romances behind
      the silver screen
between lovers too
modern for the
      golden age.

I am the desperate
      hope to be seen,
to be adored, to
      be acclaimed.

I am the pedestal
of which all
false idols must
climb, with the
delusion of flight
in their sights—
      only to be inches
      away from the sun
before they fall.

The Pacific

I AM the strength you
      wish you had—
the depths you can
never hope to understand.
When you hear the roaring
of my tide— you will
      know power.
You may think you can
tame me from my
serene surface— but it is
what's underneath that
      will pull you in
and drown you in siren
desires. You should
know better than to try
and hold me.

Santa Monica Pier

I AM the endless cadence of
        footsteps— the incessant
sound of walking away that
still echos inside your mind—
I am the empty winds
howling between the beams
of the ferris wheel— ever turning—
doomed to repeat the
same old pattern of rising
        and falling.
I am the distant shore
seen from the oval window
of the plane overhead. I am the
longing of hundreds—
the illusion of perfect
        sunshine—
the reflection of
her face staring out at
six thousand feet above the earth
and aching to know what
it would feel like to rise
        and to fall.
to rise and
        to fall.

to rise
        and to fall.

34.0083° N
118.4988° W

The Ones you leave Behind

We are the silent judges,
      the whispered wonderings,
the ones you
      left behind—
the ones you
      barely recognize
upon your return.
We look at you with
glassy vision— seeing
only the version of
you that existed before.
      The one we were
comfortable with.
      We tell you about
the wild things happening
in the miles outside this
town, this state, this country,
and we don't even
      realize that you
      are one of them.
We want you— we
need you— to think the
way we think,
      speak the way
we speak, love the
      way we love—
      because if we
are forced to consider

any deviations from
our scripted lives—
then we will be
inclined to ask questions,
      and learn that
not everything can
be perfectly defined
      and understood.
We might learn that
      we are not entitled

to this world— but
      a breathing part
of it. We might have
to learn compassion
is more than thoughts
      and prayers.
We might have to
      open our minds—
but we're afraid.
We cannot let you change,
because we
will never let ourselves
      change.

34.0092° N
118.4929° W

I-Five North

I AM rumbling pavement
and piles of discarded debris
     covered by
blooming bougainvillia—
I am voices ringing out
from open windows—
          music blaring
and sunglasses reflecting
red brake lights— I am
stop and go traffic, a skyline
in the distance— a bright
sun beaming down— piercing
through tinted windshields to
engulf you in warmth.
I steal away time— but
         some days—
you don't mind.

Locals Only

You are a stranger here
    but once,
unknown amongst
    the hum of conversation
and glasses clinking—
wanting to speak
    but never knowing
how to fill the
    silence. A starless sky—
overhead, strings of amber
    lights. Glances from
across the room— no one
cares to see you.
You are a stranger
    here
but once—
    you are
a stranger to yourself
    always.

The Musician

I AM the song you cannot have,
the dream you cannot awake
    from—
I am the voice from the radio
    that holds you
in surround sound but
never whispers in your ear—
    seemingly
within arms reach— teasing
closeness— blocks away—
heart racing, mind chasing,
feet standing still— your heart
calls to me but I will never
    know your name.
No matter how loudly you belt
    lyrics out the car window,
no matter how you feel like
    you understand the meaning
behind the words— how you
feel you could understand me—
you can never deny the
    truth—
the truth that convinces
you to skip to the next
track and roll up the
window— the truth
    that we will spend
our entire lives, nothing

        more than nonexistent
        to each other.
Don't you know
        how foolish you are
        to look for me on
        every street corner?
Don't you know—
        even if we were to
            cross paths—
if we were
to lock eyes— all I would do
            is look away?

34.0615° N
118.3089° W

Vide Noir

I have stolen every star
from the horizon and
      beyond—
casting them in stone and
laying them down to rest,
      paving the
way for wandering souls
to lead them from this
world— into the next,
      to a place where
the darkest sliver of a
winding street cuts
through the hills
      like a river,
      covered
in the nebulous glow of
shimmering marquees and
flickering streetlamps.
Where the nights are
never-ending and there
is no need for a compass
      or map.
Where one must surrender
      all knowing and
hold on tight to the hand
of fate— allowing her to
lead you to the angels who
wait.

34.1016° N
118.3267° W

The Coffee Shop

You hear the symphony
of footsteps across
stone floor, pleasantries
and assured coffee orders,
espresso machines steaming
and pounding and
ice rattling and
    you sit still,
in the corner, as the sun
peeks out from a three
day storm to burn across
your neck as the latte
crafted in your name
burns down your
throat just the same.

You hear the laughter
of a familiar soul you
must have called home
    lifetimes ago
and in a city
full of strangers and
angels and every lost
thing in between—
    you feel known.

The Hidden Artists

I AM among you— yet you could
　　　hardly tell. I am the
guitar stumbling through
chords late into the night
despite having work
in the morning.

I am the choreo
moving through the
body of every other waiter
and busboy and barista
as they cook and clean and
pull shots of espresso
to a 4/4 rhythm. I am the
vibrato that goes undiscovered,
the eyes who see cadmium yellow
in every ray of sunlight
piercing through the palm
fronds, but never has time
to pick up a paintbrush.

I am the persisting glow
coming from a window
at three in the morning
because that is the
time of the night when
these hidden artists
stir and create and

   fall apart.
I am desperation and hunger
   and persistence—
I am the will to spend
the rest of this life
fighting for a chance to express
   one's soul
to the very society that would
rather sell it off for a profit.

Eros

THE idea of everlasting
love never had any meaning
until him. His wings wrap
around his shoulders in
stillness and stretch to brush
across my skin as he gently
falls asleep beside me.

Cradled in moonlight, I watch
his eyelids flutter as his dreams
take him far away. I wonder
where he's gone. I wonder if
he'll remember. I wonder if he
might take me along next time.

In his waking hours, the days
are long and the path unsure—
he often feels so lost. It's selfish
of me, for I never feel lost when
he's near.

I'm heedless for allowing
myself to be seen as a beautiful
thing and only hoping he feels
just as magnificent in the
ardent reflection of my eyes.

I feel as if I can never give him
half as much as he offers the world.
What I have is pathetic compared to the
compassion and kindness he gives
to me so freely.

It was— after all— his kiss,
his golden arrows, that revived
my heart, and I can't
remember
if I said thank you.

Lumière Cinématographe

I AM the yearning
to be remembered—
to be inescapably captured—
the human need to
      surpass mortality
and become something
that lasts. I will be
what is cherished and
      sneered at
in the end— all grain
and dust and moments
in motion to showcase
the ordinary as eternal
and in the same breath—
ceasing death from being
our one uniting
      absolution.

LAX

I am the possibilities
you dream of every
moment you feel
trapped— I am
      the stranger
you long for
      the lover
catching your eye
from across the room—
beckoning you closer.
I am never the
same two days
in a row— I am
restlessness—
      the feeling
of being lost in
      a city where
no one knows your
name. I am your
insatiable craving—
      untouchable
and unattainable—
I will disappoint
      you and
satisfy you in the
same minute—
      I will take
you far away

and I will bring
you home. I am
the one you've
been waiting for
    all your life
and I will never
    be yours
    for long.

The Abbey

I AM the clouds of smoke
rolling over the crowd
to caress every hand
outstretched to heaven—
trying to catch the melody
or some sense of belonging.
For a moment you can feel
it— when a stranger asks
you to dance and you
shake your head— the
gravity and weightedness
of choosing yourself.
It is only the music— it is only
                       you.

Familiar faces smile
as they breathe in
each note and in this instance—
       nothing
in the world could make you
feel lonely.

A Caged Bird Set Free

NOT so long ago, she was
trapped, encased in a golden
cage made of lies so terribly
convincing that
        she stayed.

For a while, she even forgot
how to fly. She was told
behind bars was where she should
be— how normal it is to
feel trapped, and stuck,
and she'd been there for
so long she didn't know how
        to leave.

It was a voice so quiet,
growing louder with every
warm sunrise— that something
        wasn't right.
A creature such as she was
made to fly. She had
to learn— on her own— she
never needed that cage. It was a
notion she had long
        outgrown.

Look at her now!

Soaring,
      piercing through
layers of the atmosphere
like a bullet unleashed.

She's wild,
      untamed, and
nothing will ever be able to
lock her behind closed
      doors again.

Boats Against the Current

THE green light calls like
an unreachable truth—
one you could spend
a lifetime wading through—
      dark oceans
        and icy mist
drench over your skin—
you allow it to soak you
through and through.

You transfix on the beacon—
hoping it will reveal any answers
      it may hold.
Watch as the light signals to the
      stars, the moon,
but never to you. Like so many
others— this is a language you
cannot understand— you try to
interpret the meaning of the
emerald beams but it never
quite makes sense.
      Regardless—
you walk away believing in
something you don't understand—
      and that gives you hope.

Paris

SUMMER 2023

The Only Stars Visible in the City of Light

There is a moment
before you round the corner —
when you think maybe
my stars won't shine
     after all.
Maybe pitch-darkness
     is all that can
be found under this
     void of a sky.
This is the moment
     I need you to
believe in me all
     the more—
with everything you
     are— believe
and I will burn
for you—
in twenty thousand
sparkling bulbs like
     moonlight breaking
itself across
     ocean waves—
I will come alive
     and you will
stare in awe— without
     a single thought
of mere milky ways
or tired constellations—

you will see me as
        a beacon and
never again will you
        search for
            the northern star.

La Dame de Fer

Poets gather in the grass to capture
some sort of beauty—
      the sun
sinks below the horizon,
illuminating their inspiration
as a spotlight would shine
upon a star actress on
      stage.
They all gaze in awe
of her magnificence, wondering
what it must be like to be so
      adored.
Hoping— one day—
to feel just as significant.

48.8584° N
2.2945° E

Les Échos du Passé

For eight centuries I have endured,
your lady of seven sorrows—
my stone grotesques have gazed
down at you night and day—
reminding you of your own
mortality— my heart, a
rose window— shining despite
the damage it has withstood.
My spired fingers reaching
towards heaven may
have been burned but
do not be fooled— I will
      reach again,
I will feel the hands of god
through the laborers who
      restore me—
just as when they built these walls
for the first time so long ago.
      Tell all those
      who behold me—
not even the fires of hell itself
can extinguish my holiness.

The Poet of Notre Dame

FINGERS typing on an old
crimson typewriter, the
wind blows from one
artist to the next—
      wrapping
us all in inspiration.
Poets race words
across pages— gold ink
and fountain pen and
typewritten with letters
as black as the night sky—
he speaks of sanctuary in
a language I can only barely
comprehend— but that
doesn't matter so much—
for when he looks into
my eyes— I understand
      every word.

La Nuit Étoilée, 1888

I AM ochre light
    shining across
cobblestones reflecting
in the eyes of
    lovers.
I am shadows,
    violet and sapphire,
settling in alleyways
and stretching across
a velvet horizon.
I am sunburst
stars that are so much
more than bright dots
on a blue-black
canvas— I am
jewels of ruby, emerald,
    topaz— if only
you would look closer.
If only you would
see me— truly,
know me— utterly.
I am more than
    light and dark—
I am a world of color
you have yet to
    touch.

48.8600° N
2.3266° E

À Vous de Jouer, Gare de l'est

You may never see my face—
as the masses rush by— but
throughout these bright halls—
you will hear my unmistakable
song piercing through the
      noise.
Ink and ivory. Many will never
look up from their feet, nor
screens, nor will they seek out
      to find me—
yet I will be heard nonetheless.
Whether you care or not— I will
continue to sing for you— and
all the indifferent travelers
who pass through this
      place.
For my chords were crafted
to be heard— even if no one
cares to listen.

Thunderstorms in Tuileries Garden

You have abandoned me. The
sky is roaring— lightning breaks
midnight into pieces, and you
have all left me. Scurried away
in fear of rushing floods down
stone staircases and perilous rivers
where pathways used to be.
My trees silhouette ebony
against the backdrop of
polished city streets.
Puddles form into lakes and
if you're not careful you
could fall into another
      world.
And yet— those who dare
to enter here will find something
that can never be found
when the sun is ablaze—
something so rare it is
      hard to believe.
It could even be said
a few souls bold enough or
      desperate enough
seek me out only when
it's pouring down rain
just to find the only place
in this whole godforsaken town
where one can truly be

alone.

48.8635° N
2.3275° E

The Watercolorist

I am the brushstrokes lost under
layers of labored soul—
the old sketch covered
     by new ideas—
secrets never revealed
past one set of tired
         eyes still
   searching
for meaning—
I am an idea
     unspoken—
I am an empty belly
and sore feet and
blue and green and
         red fingers—
   I am the longing to
be seen and understood by
     something other
     than
     an old mirror
whose reflection
I've gazed into
a thousand
    times
and never
    come to know
any better.

48.8526° N
2.3471° E

L'île aux Oiseaux

W<small>E</small> enter to feel the
        time
that passes—
in a place not made
        for us,
but for the winged ones,
the helpless ones,
the brave ones, the
creatures we long
        to be—
to understand
how it must feel to
taste the sky, to
see the earth melt
away below our feathers,
and with it—
        we imagine
all our worries might
        melt away too.

48.8631° N
2.3047° E

59 Rue de Rivoli

I AM a secret labyrinth
tucked away, reaching
floor by floor upwards to
some kind of
      heaven.
As you get lost in
my corridors you will
be filled with more
questions than
      answers.
You will crawl through
the eyes of each artist
and for a
      moment—
you'll see the world as they
do. As if you enter their very
skin and for a split second
you are them—
      until
you blink or turn your head—
and the furious rhythm of the
streets sends you crashing back
into this realm— forever longing
to be someone else.
      Someone
who can see the world as
      something
more than this.

Renaissance Boy

You must have been a past-life
lover, or my heart wouldn't
sink like this when you
      glance towards me
for the first time with those
pale eyes. We are surrounded
by pigment and strangers and roars
of the city, but when you
      look at me—
for a fraction of a second—
all is still and silent.
You see right through me,
as only an artist can.
I can't help but wonder
in what lifetimes I've known
you— and in what lifetime
I might see you
      again.

48.8592° N
2.3456° E

Temple de l'Amour

If you could truly know
      me— you would
never again feel lonely.
      Look how the
flowers toss and turn
toward each other in the
breeze— can you
      feel the trees
reaching for the
sun as you reach
for everyone who
      ever left you?
Settle down in
the thick carpet
of dewy grass
      and let
me caress you—
      let me shelter you
while you wait for
      the return of
the one you have
      lost. Ascend
these stones and hope—
look into my eyes and
pray. And if
he never comes,
let me hold you
      through the night—

for isn't love,
        in the end,
all that keeps you
              alive?

Midsummer Muses

We are the quiet ones,
in a sea of noise—
our breath soft as
a french perfume,
toes in the grass and
eyes darting from sky
to page— the sound
of ink pen and paintbrush
sweeping across blank
space— we are the
observers, the memory
keepers, the admirers, the
seers of unnoticeable things—
we are the artists— and in
the midst of chaos, we are
tranquility.

Jardin Tino Rossi

FOREIGN and familiar music
washes over each clasped
hand and sun-soaked shoulder—
foxtrot, salsa, tango, waltz—
dancing couples fill the
amphitheater with purpose as
the Seine flows by. Wide and
flat boats skim along with
children waving from the
top deck. A woman blows
smoke over her shoulder to
create the misty clouds that
hang so low above Paris.
  Here—
it must always be summer evening,
with wind blowing soft soft soft through
drooping willow branches, never harsh,
never cold. Even in the winter—
this place must be
  filled with warmth.

Lovers on the Terrace

We are Rodin's *Le Basier*
come to life beneath
the shade of manicured
trees— as if bronze and
marble could
      breathe
just to wrap arms around
each other and tilt heads
      for a kiss.
It is only in this city of love
where ancient art may
come to life and walk among
      the modern cynics—
causing us to turn our heads,
to rethink for a moment
      that maybe
the love we've dreamed of
and cast aside isn't so
impossible after all.

Let them live Quietly

NEARLY 400 years old— I have
seen dozens of reigns and
the falling of kings— I have
stood as war has raged
around me and I have
sheltered lovers from
the bright sun—
      today
I am a sanctuary for
strangers, regulars, and
the smallest of winged
creatures. Past Adonis and
Aphrodite I see a savage
      little child—
      in my years,
I've come to learn, all children
are heartless until they grow
older and obtain the burden
      of caring.
She chases innocent ducklings
with a leaf— she throws
it. Picks up another leaf—
      chases—
throws it. The poor creatures
scatter. Her mother does
      nothing.
I wish I could cast her feet in stone
to hold her in place—

keep her still— keep them safe.
Then an old man steps in front
of her and protests in two
languages. *No, no,*
ça suffit maintenant.
Let them live quietly.
I can't help but think we all
need such a protector— and
as the people ebb and flow—
my waters, like a wish, will
        echo,
Let them live quietly.

Le Jardin de Sacré Couer

POETS gather at the top
of Montmartre— as
they always have— to
listen and be enchanted.
How lucky we are
to be a part of a city
that celebrates art.

How lucky I am
to lead them here,
to guide them
through verses, and
to show them to
inspiration. Artistic
passion radiates
from these streets—
and I can't help but
feel as though I've
lived this all before.

Wall of Love

IF you feel unheard— unknown—
maybe even a little alone—
in a city where you don't know
the language— where you feel
like no one is listening—
        come to me.
No matter who you are
or where you are from
you will hear one phrase
echoed across 311 languages.
Ti tengu caru, Σε αγαπώ, Je t'aime,
मैं आपसे प्यार करती हूँ, Ayóó'áníínísh́ní,
Is breá liom tú, Te amo, 사랑해요,
Aku mencintaimu, 愛してるよ,
Ich liebe dich, اُحِبُّك, Nakupenda,
আমি তোমায় ভালোবাসি, Ti amo,
Я тебя люблю, aukaglyo, Tôi yêu bạn,
Rwy'n dy garu di, Te iubesc, Jeg elsker deg,
Szeretlek, Ik houd van je, Ke a go rata…
come here, come here and find
the words that speak to your
heart, the words you will
always long for and search
for and smile when you
        hear them—
come to me and know
that I love you,
        I love you,
    I love you.

48.8848° N
2.3386° E

Artist 64

I AM quiet, surrounded
      by nothingness,
an arm reaching upward,
holding on to a single balloon
      taking me away
from the deafening crowds
below— I am a dream
hovering above a man,
      graphite shadows
and watercolor clouds.

I am strangers captured
in pigment, in ink—
a soft *bonjour* and kind
      eyes.
A shrug, a little laugh,
a sincere *merci*—
and a hope, a wish by
the name of *maybe you'll*
find the explanation
      yourself.

48.8865° N
2.3408° E

Always & Always

BESIDE me, a
mother's skirts flow
like Monet's waterlilies and
her daughter laughs in
the same way a hydrangea
blooms— bold and with
all her being. I'd like to say
I'm somehow like
soft yellow irises or a
serene field of tulips—
but that would
        be a lie—
I look at a singular
        wild rose
growing behind iron
bars and I see an
image of me—
covering myself
in thorns and
reaching out—
begging to be
        held.

Rome

SUMMER 2022

Coins in a Fountain

I AM roaring waterfalls and
humming crowds— I am
grand and timeless and
I am what brings
you back— each time—
like a lighthouse calling
a boat to shore— gold
and silver coins call
you home. If home
is where the heart is—
then your heart is
                    mine.
As you toss the euro
over your right shoulder,
                you smile—
surrounded by people who
can still believe in something.

The Harpist

S<small>UNLIGHT</small> as a spotlight, I am
a fallen angel that must be from
the heaven they all
      speak of—
      a melody
to surround you in holiness
as you aimlessly wander
ancient paths. I am peace
in havoc, giving away a piece
of my soul in every note
you hear. I may no longer be
      immortal
but this song I can share will
live forever in the whispering
of these trees, the birds
continuing my refrains
      long after
      I'm gone—
carrying the tune
of this eternal city
      and the next.

Terrazza Viale del Belvedere

I AM wrought iron bars to keep
you safe— a bird's eye view of
the beast below. I hold you inches away
from reaching your arms upward
and grasping the ether itself.

I am all the love and hope in the world
stored in one little brass lock carved
      with a pair of initials
by thin hands and tear-stained
fingertips— I am the ghost of
who you used to be standing
only a few feet away,
turning her head
towards the sunlight—

trying to remember what
it's like to feel anything at all.

41.9096° N
12.4800° E

The Rambling Man

I am old, dusty, charcoal-leather shoes
crushed by old, tanned, dirt-covered
      heels—
I am stumbling chords
and stubborn sincerity.
I may not have the smooth
voice of an crooner— I may not
be a master of melody— but
that will never silence me.
    Even after this
soil swallows me whole and
fills my lungs with
      silt—
the echo of my
wretched song will
haunt in your ears,
    forever
        out of tune.

The Nameless Woman

I am the unnoticed one, the
woman you walk right by
because she is too broken and too
sad and far too insignificant to
gaze upon. I am your mother,
your sister, your daughter. I am
every day she has spent smiling
despite the pain— I am her
nerve and commitment to show
her face when all she wants to
do is hide away. You will
never travel thousands of miles
to see me, you will never tell your
lover about me or write me into
stories— I will forever and only be
exactly as I am in this lifetime—
stone-cold and forgotten.

41.9115° N
12.4797° E

Roman Cafe, 2022

Happy to be happened upon—
welcoming weary travelers
with open arms, a soft gesture,
two fresh servings of spaghetti—
something so ordinary, it shouldn't
matter at all. But for those
who are tired— a moment of
kindness can change an
               entire demeanor.
Maybe it is these tiny, seemingly
unimportant moments between
all the paramount events
that actually matter
               most of all.

Stargazers

I AM eyes turned toward the dark skies above as a sea of gleaming lights stretches out below— I am pure awe over Cygnus and Ursa Major and Ophiuchus— I am hands held and poems recited as one voice under a moon-colored street lamp— I am attentive ears and wishes made in turquoise fountains, I am a white rose to say 'I am worthy of you'— I am a bouquet to say 'thank you for seeing me'— I am hearts worn on the outside of chests and absolute weightlessness. I am the assurance there is magic and wonder to be found in each moment— if only it may be sincerely sought after.

Galileo

You could easily
pass me by—
      another old
man in another old city—
but if time is forgotten
and walls can be broken
down with a smile, then
will you walk with
me for a while?
      A quiet,
slow stroll under umbrella
pine trees, past Goethe,
to a tiny temple often
unseen, overlooked.
      Though
I may not be here for long,
please believe that paths
must cross for a reason,
      and I
am better for having
known you at all.

Tavolo 40

I AM every head turning
      as you walk in, I am
your favorite antipasti, your
favorite primi piati, your
favorite dessert— the best
      tiramisu
you've ever tasted.
I am innocent love poems
scribbled and giggled over
about the endearing Roman boy
still getting used to his new glasses
and this unnatural July heat.
Her paynes grey, french
ultramarine eyes search for his
      across the room.
      There is a hum
that fills and spills out onto the
dimly lit strada, but you can always
hear her voice so clear. If there is
one thing for certain, you feel
      at home here.

Leaving the Past Behind

I SEE glimpses of her— like veiled memories making their way out of my subconscious and into view. Singing sad ballads in that crammed cafe, charting stars, ignoring the Mouth of Truth, dancing on that old bridge with a boy she'll never see again, running circles around the Colosseum at sunrise, being pulled on a train just as the doors close. Laughing with forsaken friends. Sailboats in the distance, an impossible blue, sun-soaked village streets that have known me, hidden paths on winding cliffsides that have long since forgotten me. Echoes of my former selves live in every corner of this place. She crosses the threshold of this station for the first time. She runs into the clear water, she throws herself from a jagged cliff— she resurfaces with a smile on her lips, she wanders tiny alleyways and climbs the steepest stairs two at a time— her lungs heave for air. She bites into a fresh apricot and lays back on that pebble beach— dreaming of the woman she hopes to be. And as I look back at her, still laying in the sun— I wonder if she can feel me at all, as I disappear through a long tunnel— away from her— away from Rome and the sapphire coast— perpetually facing forward— never able to gaze on the past for too long before it starts to burn.

44.0990° N
9.7375° E

Edinburgh

WINTER 2022

Princes Street Gardens

I AM snowdrops shivering
in a February breeze—
    winding pathways
reflecting downturned
eyes, mist falling from
the hands of muses reaching
out towards a sea
    of grey clouds.
I am three white birch trees
holding up the sky
with spindly fingers—
I am fushia branches
swaying in the wind—
biding their time
until we can all bloom—
I am tiny feet jumping
in puddles and
hot breath swirling
    in cold air.
I am the bricked
gardener's cottage
surrounded in a
kind of silence
that should never be
able to exist in
the heart of
    a city
    this big—

I am timeless—
I am reverence— where you
can you lose yourself and find
you can be in any time,
anywhere in the world, be
anyone you please— until
you cross that iron fence
and return to reality.

The Old Man of the Blue Bookshop

I AM Charon to a river
of words, I am quiet and
precise and I know every
title that overflows from
these towering shelves.
Where one may see
        disorder—
I see a thousand different
worlds— a thousand
opportunities to listen
to someone other than
the incessant voice
        inside your head.
A thousand chances to
understand another
point of view.
I am the birth and
death of these
very pages.
I am offering an
escape of empathy
in a society
that aims only
to ensnare you
        in apathy.

55.9460° N
3.2016° W

Royal Mile

I AM raindrops cascading down
unfamiliar eyes as the frigid
tears of mid-winter.
I am hidden passageways
and endless twilight—
dark shadows stretching
        themselves
across cobblestone
roads like soldiers in
        line—
history seeping
through cracks of stone
        the color
of aging parchment—
bells sounding in the
distance and every head
        turning.
You will never know
quite where
I begin or end.

Edinburgh Cafe, 2022

Soft hum of conversation.
Lovers smile and look down
into their steaming cups.
A little boy leans over to
watch the artist sketch.
The pale woman with espresso
eyes clears the table. Mugs clink.
Front door creaks. Packets of
sugar are torn in two. Rain
slides down the dirty window—
a river forms in the center
of the street. Cream walls flake.
Strangers' eyes never meet—
reflections ignored in mirrors
on the wall. A chill held
in four corners.

The Professor

An old felt hat in the same
hand as a silver topped
cane. The way he tells me
"You just have to keep
writing— every day,
      no matter what
      anyone says."
reminds me of the professor
who first gave me poetry.
And maybe he is you—
for a moment— saying,
"Rachel, you just
      have to keep writing."
These words sure do feel
like yours, they beat
inside me like a second
heart— *you just*
have to keep writing.
His folded tartan scarf
matches the crinkles by
his eyes when he says,
"The secret to writing poetry
      is to have a soul
           on fire."
In this moment
his voice is your voice,
his eyes are your eyes,
and it is as if you are

dismissing me from class—
sending all your
      young poets
out into the wild world
with a simple word
of encouragement—
      for the last time.

The Seabirds

I am strong white wings
turned grey and brown
from the ceaseless rain—
I am hungry mouths and
searching eyes, I am
unbridled and soaring—
      for this is all I know.
What is it like
spending your whole
life on the ground?
Does obeying gravity make
your worries weigh
      you down?
The curvature
of the earth reveals
the meaning of life. It's
a shame you never
      look up.

Horoscope for Diana

BORN of earth and Tuscan
sun— a decade spent
      in cold rain.
An unknown sea held
within— uncharted—
yet to be explored.
Time passes all too suddenly.
Dreams keep on flying by—
as tricky to catch as
      falling leaves.
Eyes shed cherry blossom
tears and suddenly it is
      spring again.
Another year— come and
lost— searching,
hoping, breaking, too far
gone and yet to begin.
Will she ever reach
      satisfaction?

55.9504° N
3.1885° W

The Lovers

I am four bouquets
of roses and a teenage
couple holding each other
    while waiting
for the bus. I am shared
popcorn and giggling over
a glass of wine. I am any
excuse to touch his shoulder
    or her wrist.
I am the concerned old man
carefully helping the love of
his life inch down the
stairs. I am the tapping
foot of the boy waiting
    for the girl
to come back— wondering
what to say next. I am first
date jitters and the comfort
of knowing every wrinkle
    by her eyes.
I am everywhere you
look— and nowhere
to be found.

55.9472° N
3.1970° W

The Addicts

I AM the swirling
smoke from your lungs—
bellowing out through
crisp air in clouds of
relief. I am a triple
shot of espresso— an
orange bottle— an earthy
scent seeping under
doorways, another open tab—
the look in the eyes of an
unrequited lover. I am
unshakable, uncontrollable,
      insatiable—
I am attached to every
person passing by— in
some way, some shape,
some form,
      someone
will always be chasing
          a high.

55.9516° N
3.2037° W

The Lothians

I AM blood
    pulsing,
        coursing,
pumping through
the veins
    of this dark city.
Monday morning
    I am
        rushed
and dreaded and
    delayed
    and needed.
In the middle
    of the night,
the rain, the long
        winter—
I am still
    here
to collect you,
    to hold you,
to take you
        away,
    to let you
            go.

Roseburn Terrace

I AM overlooked,
overgrown—
crocus & primrose
blooming in February
    cold—
I am the sound of a string
    intrument tuning
through closed windows,
spiral stone stairs, barking
behind Blythe, Smith screaming
again, the red door on the
groundfloor remains
    nameless.
I am off-key singing
from the pub across
street, outpouring with
spilled light and the
unmistakeable scent of
    overflowing
pint after pint after—
the sunlight cannot make it
through the fog and the
never-ceasing wind pounds
against the old panes.
You wake as
    tired
as when you lulled
    to sleep—

and all that's left
is a bit of warmth
and a hollow creak
in an empty bed.

55.9461° N
3.2344° W

London

WINTER 2022
SUMMER 2023

St. Dunstan-in-the-East

Tucked out of sight,
silent as a prayer—
I am stone remains
of great fire and blitz and
terror. I am no longer
      a shelter
             but a shell.
I am bare vines
covering once stained
glass— I am steadfast,
indomitable, yellow
      star-flowers—
I am twisted tree branches
reaching towards the
clouds like elderly
      fingers.
I am the air of winter,
summer, autumn, spring—
blazing sun and
torrential rain through
      always
             open doors.
I am eternal life
after almost certain
death— I am
heaven itself,
      enduring.

51.5097° N
0.0825° W

Song of Trafalgar Square

A HUNGRY guitar strumming—
craving to be heard.
I am the voice weaving
its way through crowds and
noise to find you— I wrap you
in familiarity as you
      wade through
the unknown of city streets.

Before you know it, you find
yourself singing along—
lips barely moving— *and I
won't ever let you go.*
In a few short steps
you will be out of sight,
I will be out of mind, but
this song will go on—
      day after day—
as another, inevitably,
takes my place.

The Impressionists, Room 44

FROM grade school art
lessons, to sitting
in the same room
    with Degas,
Monet, Pissarro, Cézanne—
I ask them how to look at
the world and see something
worth staying for.
They show me flooded
rivers, snowy trees, women
flying through the
air in trapeze— I
see brushstrokes of
color that could only ever
exist in their eyes and wonder
what makes their version of
this world feel so different
    from reality?
I look into their canvases
and wonder if we, as
observers only, are a
    lost cause.
I look at my plaintive reflection
in the protective glass
and wonder the same.

Kyoto Garden

Stepping stones descend
into murky waters—
the home of
sunset-colored koi—
     swishing
through the pond
like birds in flight.
A fervant wind
throws itself against
     every limb—
movement brings
these sleeping trees
to life. Bare branches
swaying— bright pink
shoots bursting from
     old growth—
a waxing moon peeks through
the early evening sky.
The laughter here
casts itself like ripples
     across still water—
there is serenity to be seen
in golden leaves touched
by the dying rays of the sun—
if an eden can be found
in London, this
     must be it.

Paddington

A LOW rumbling welcomes
travelers as they
flee in and out of train
cars like bees from
    a hive—
running, chasing, reaching
for doors just as they
    close
    sighs of relief from
those who made it
    sighs of frustration
from those left behind.
Tears and smiles
accompany every
hello and goodbye—
a young man rushes
by with a bouquet
    of wilting flowers—
I wonder which he
    will be saying today—
hello or goodbye—
    that seems
    to be all
that is ever said
    in train stations—
hello,
    goodbye,
    hello, goodbye—

maybe that's why
travelers like me who have
such a hard time standing still
always seem to feel
most at home in a place
we can never claim
as our own.

Hope Speaks to the Hesitant

I am the moment
you realize things
might be changing
    for the better.
I am hundreds of smiles
illuminated—
I am a musical
thread of human
    connection
tying every heart
in the room
    together.
I am ephermal—
which makes you sad.
I am the reason,
on this brief night,
you believe in
something good.

Song in Covent Garden

W̲H̲E̲N̲ the thrill of the night
winds down and shop
windows go dark—
I am all that is left.
I am *someone like you*
and *all of me* and
voices that have never
spoken to each other
suddenly sing together
without a second thought—
a cold breeze blows through
green arches as they
look, really look, into
unfamiliar faces—
        and smile.

The Perfect Stranger

I AM a face you will forget—
a name you will never know.
I am an entire universe that
will pass you by— a mosaic
of stories and sorrows that
are never meant for your ears.
I am everything you want— for
when you look at me, I can be
whoever you need me to be.
I can't be anything otherwise—
for in this lifetime, we were
never slated to be
        anything more
                than almost.

51.5233° N
0.0755° W

The Gloucester Arms

I AM glowing fluorescent
candles— I am the kind
eyes of a bartender
keeping watch over his
      domain.
I am the cool night air
rushing in each time
the wooden door
swings open. Leather
chairs, scratched and worn,
hold patrons in place
as full glasses press
      against lips.
I am the hum of
conversation and the
piercing laugh of a drunken
man. Clock hands tick
on the wall but no
one pays any mind.

Time may pass here—
but for one reason
      or another—
it can't be felt.

51.4982° N
0.1839° W

Old Flame

I AM the lantern burning from three
or three thousand miles away—
I am the bit of longing
that will never fully
        dissipate.
Eyes speaking more
than words ever could—
keeping him at arms length
when all you want
is to pull him closer.
Not knowing quite how
to say what you want
so you write
this poem
        instead.
Spending the next
long while wondering
what it'd be like in a
different life. Stopping yourself
from dwelling because
that somehow
hurts more than
        leaving.
Looking over your shoulder
in the rain. Staring at lips.
Wondering what it
would feel like
        to stay.

The Actor

I AM a siren call
for those who wish
to be understood.
I am hot spotlights
and a voice reaching
out over hundreds
of darkened faces.

I am thunderous
applause and hesitant
first steps out on
stage. I am Icarus and
I am the sun.
The storyteller and
the beacon.

I am here for a
moment, gone in
an instant— fated to
live in memory
forever— fated to
repeat the same
words again and
again— until everyone
has a chance
to hear them.

Poets' Corner

You stand before me to see Keats,
Austen, Shelley, and Olivier— but
can you hear me?
I am the voices that will
never fade— I am
Carroll's question ringing
through rose windows,
"Is all our life then, but a
                            dream?"
I am Byron rattling around in
your ribcage, "But there is
               that within me
     which shall tire
torture and time,
       and breathe when
            I expire."
I am born again when you
read my poem and die
when you forget my name.
Regardless, my words will
       remain—
echoing among these
teardrop chandeliers
and vaulted ceilings,
finding themselves
in a stranger's mouth as long as
the stars burn high above— with
       Larkin on your lips,

"Our almost-instinct
almost true:
    What will survive of
        us is love."
and as you walk away, bound
to barely remember this place—
you hear the Bronte's whisper,
"With courage to endure, with
courage to endure, with courage
        to endure."

East-facing Window

I AM the ebb and flow
of rail cars passing through
Waterloo Station— carrying tired
creatures to and from their
        homes.
Midnight is creeping closer— like
the blue topped train pulling into
the platform—
        pausing for a
               moment—
resting as the light-filled
things settle in— and then
        continuing on.

It seems every star
        has been plucked
from the night to settle
in each towering
window on the skyline.

For what is a star, after all,
        but a bright soul burning
              from so far away?

51.5010° N
0.1167° W

Holland Park

WINDING passageways
offer a refuge
from defined city blocks.
    Here,
a place untouched
by time— walls stand
centuries old
and roses bloom
in the dead of
    winter.
A pair of peacocks roam freely,
bright blue and green feathers,
with eyes that see straight
    through you—
they know a language you wish
    to understand.
A language of
assurance and
    confidence—
these are creatures who know exactly
what they are here to do
    with their lives.
Existing moment
    to moment.
Resting when they are tired,
wandering when they
long for something new—
never caring too much

about being anywhere
        other than this moment.
I look at the two
old men playing chess
and I see identical
        contentment.
I look at myself in the reflection
of rippling waters and wish
        I could see the same.

Another English Pub

I AM clinking glasses
and dimmed lights
and a kiss on the
cheek from an
old flame gone cold—
a smile from a stranger
and pushing past streams
of people to the bar.
I am eight pints in and
inconsolable laughter.
Whether it is a moment,
a minute, or hours together—
some nights you wish
to last far longer
than they ever could.

Goodbyes never get
any easier and walking
out into the cold
always makes
you wish for
a hand
to hold.

Cruel to be Kind

I AM the 3am doubt that
creeps into your mind midday—
    poisoning your
thoughts and making you
question why you ever
stepped outside your
front door in the first
place. I am the lies told
to you through smiles,
the eyes that actively
avoid meeting yours,
the un-invitations— the
silent I've-had-enough-of-you
for-today half hugs. The stark
truth that haunts—
nobody actually cares
    if you're here or not.

The Enchanted Bookstore

FIND solace here.
Wooden shelves overflowing
with countless words—
you are surrounded by voices
yet submerged in
    silence.
This is a place where you
don't feel so alone.
I am the only remaining
threshold for thoughts and
ideas of generations
    passed.
I am the offering of stories
ancient and new,
to see you through til
    tomorrow—
to make the hardest
parts of life
    bearable.
I am quiet and I am
    deafening.
I am a portal to
a million other
worlds and I will always
be here,
    waiting,
for when you need
    relief.

51.5204° N
0.1520° W

Artists admiring Artists

How you crane your
neck from pen to
painting—
how you sit still
       and stare—
how you fidget
to find comfort as
the world around you
       disappears
and time stops.
Artists can't help but flock to
museums like this—
       to glimpse
into the past and
search for
meaning.
In every carved statue
an emotion is
uncovered— a life lived—
a moment in time
captured and made
       to live forever.
Do these artists know
how beautiful
       they are?
Breathing
beneath carved
          angels—

works of art
          themselves.
I can't help but
marvel at
          both.
Standing here— surrounded
by masterpieces—
          some
never having lived,
          and some
               so briefly alive.

Grave of the Unknown Warrior

UNKNOWN and yet well known,
dying and behold we live—
I am your son, your brother,
your father— your father's father—
I never wanted to be surrounded by
red poppies and stone diamonds—
I wanted to
      come home
to my love, my children, my terrible
neighbor, my favorite ceramic mug—
I wanted to hear the horns sound
as my boots hit the ground,
I wanted to march in parades—
    The War is Over
as every newspaper headline—
I wanted to put all of this behind me
and live until I was so frail I could
barely walk on my own. I wanted to
open my eyes and see the sun rise again
and again and again until I got sick of it—
I wanted to hold her hand— to
      keep her close—
I wanted a life of trivial and
intolerable things—
      but instead
for god and country,
I am buried
among the kings.

51.4994° N
0.1273° W

Summer Park Pathway, 2023

I will show
        you a glimpse
     of your past— a possibility
of your future—
sitting across
     from each other...

          To your left,
   a young couple—
early twenties—
   he lays his head
on her lap while
       she thumbs
   through the pages
of a novel.

A quiet love.

          To your right,
   an older woman—
years weighing her
   down— sitting
      at the end
of an empty bench—
   hunched over and picking
      through her lunch.

A quiet loss.

You walk
>	between them
>		and feel it all—
>	the love, the loss,
as intimately
>	as if it is your own.
Because maybe
>		it was—
>	because
>		maybe it will be.

Heaven's Gate

It makes sense— for him to
lead me here— to a space in between.
Somewhere we've always particularly
    known.
Somewhere we will never
escape from. It's beautiful here—
shattered stained glass surrounds us
and moves slowly like a leaden
kaleidoscope. A soft symphony
cushions our conversation
from the sirens in the streets. I look
into his eyes and I can't decide if
I'm seeing an old lover or an old friend—
or someone in between. Regardless,
I smile when he looks at me.

Keep the Secret locked in your Heart

I AM the gasps. I am the laughter.
I am the hushed silence—
more holy than a cathedral,
the sharing of emotion between
strangers who would normally
share nothing more than
a passing glance. I am
the curtain rising and
falling— the same night
relived 29,268 times. I
am a history of secret
keepers and lovers of mystery.
I am a thread tying
all of them together with
a promise to preserve
the plot— with the
forethought to think of others—
all for the sake of storytelling
and the shock of a moment
      unexpected.

51.5129° N
0.1276° W

Love from Kew

I am winding pathways dotted
with ancient gods and thorned
roses filling the air around you
with their intoxicating perfume. I am
centuries old glass houses holding
leaves the size of giants and
sunlight streaming through
        in sheaves of gold.
I am shy fronds folding at
        the touch of a hand.
Gaurdian water lilies made of
myth and mystique. A retreat from
the belly of the beast, the
bustling Charing Cross streets—
I am an oasis, a paradise one will
        happily get lost in.
In this torrential city—
        I am of heaven.

Innocence & Sadness

I WILL pound your bones
with bass and wrap you
     in cold night air
the same way loving arms wrap
around the couples
        beside you.
You will feel more alone than ever
and yet you will feel a part
of something so much bigger
     than yourself—
when you finally have the courage
     to sing and sing
            loud.
For the louder you
     sing— the more you
         dance—
the more people will turn to you—
will magnetize themselves
     toward you.
You will grip the hands
of a nameless girl as you sing lyrics
to each other that you both
hold so dear— that you only ever want
     others to hear.
You will look into the eyes of another
who can see the beauty in you and
for a moment, his lighthouse gaze
makes you believe in it too.

You will hold your hands to the sky,
to the stars of Aquila peeking through
the grey clouds and you will feel
the movement of those around you
      sync up to your own—
you will see puffs of smoke blown above
the crowd.
    Breath.
        You will see others'—
you will hold your own. You will feel
    alive. alive. alive.
On an evening you will
    not forget
you will feel as though,
finally,
    you belong.

Other Cities

2021 | 2022 | 2023

The Floating City

WE are the old world keeping pace
with the new— we are what it feels
like to be lost in a winding maze and
then emerge upon one sure path.
We cover ourselves in ornate masks—
      but unlike most,
we know how to remove them. To
reveal our true selves. We are glistening
glass beads catching the afternoon
sun, we are delicate as lace and
sturdy as a handmade gondola
passed through generations of
fathers and sons. We are boundless,
and endless, and no matter how far
you roam— a part of you will
      always ache to return.

The City of Fog

THEY said it was
impossible— until a
poet proved them wrong.
The steel redwood trunks
grip the ocean floor as
a mile of suspension tethers
      either shore.
You lean your head out the window
as the car speeds forward
and look up— the orange-red
towers disappear into the fog.
For all you know, they could
touch the fiery sun itself.

Wires descend from the
mist and hold on for
dear life as the roadway
sways with the wind.
      You smile,
for you know what it's like
to be a poet who believes
in impossible things.
      You sigh,
for you know what it's like
to be the only one in the
room left believing.

You close your eyes,

for it hurts to know
you'll never be respected,
revered, or remembered for
anything as marvelous as this.

The Secret Library

HUSHED whispers, creaky stairs—
steady breath is the rhythm
of this place. I am thought
and opinion— fact and
declaration. To be holding
more words than could ever
be spoken in a lifetime—
               I am silence.
If you close your eyes,
you will hear only
the delicate sound
of pages turning, timber settling,
footsteps wandering— and
the unmistakable presence
of the books themselves—
breathing along
with their readers.

The Docent

I am the voice of lost
voices— the eyes of a
fellow artist to show you
the grief beneath the
poppies and the alizarin
crimson that has long
since faded away.

I am the held back tears
and the deep desire to know
what lies beyond
the canvas and the keen
understanding that
some things must
remain a mystery.

I am the bridge bringing
history closer to today and
although my voice
may be but a whisper—
everytime you stand before
a grieving Van Gogh—
you will remember me.

Skeleton Crew

We are the lost ones—
those with no place
to go and nowhere
to call home.
Stranded and
stuck and tired.
Oh, so tired.
All we want is for
someone, something—
to take our hands and
guide us away— quietly,
gently— or to cradle us
in their arms and let
us sleep in safety.
Instead, we are
forgotten
between here and
there— made
to wait and never
to know for sure
if we will make
it out of this liminal
space— this place
between places,
this purgatory.

33.6361° N
84.4294° W

A Conversation for Three

M<small>E</small>
standing here wondering, gazing,
wishing, knowing I'm better off not
saying a word— the alluring eyes of
a stranger piercing through a well-worn
veil— my heart reaching out through
the bars of my rib cage, logic and
reason holding the key hostage.

You
strolling through marble streets,
Piazza Brà, searching for someone
to stop you and ask *Who are you?*
Why do you carry that green notebook
everywhere? What are you writing?
What do you see when you look at me?

And the Moon
gazing down as I watch you
walk away. Could be
lovers, never to meet.
She sighs in silver
moonbeams, cries
in falling stars, knowing
all too well the sinking
sensation of longing
for someone
you can never have.

The City of Lilies

I am the beating renaissance heart
of Tuscany, veins reaching out from
Ponte Vecchio— connecting
the city with soot-colored
cobblestones. A watery snake called
Arno cuts through me like a
blue ribbon as I tell you
the legend of the lily in a lion's
mouth. I am old hands that chisel
even older stone and eyes that
can see angels trapped in
marble. I am the soul carefully
      being set free and
thousands of strangers hoping
to gaze upon it. You are one
of these strangers, wandering,
seeking. Something here feels
familiar to you— as if a part
of you belongs to me— begging
      for you to stay.

Epilogue
After A.S.J. Tessimond

I AM beloved, forgotten, clueless, clever, anonymous Girl, stranded in the only world I know. Beckoned by a muse and defeated by doubt. Judged by my mirror, scared of my past repeating; fumbling with cold hands; longing to be Myself— whoever that may be— Reaching; self-criticized, self-aware, self-lessened; Decaying angel, weaver of grief and longing.

DEDICATIONS

*Poems in this collection are dedicated
to the following individuals:*

Gallery 548 . . . . Morgana F.
The Stonewall Inn. Cody G.
C Train: Last Stop Euclid Av . . . . Emily C. & Vanessa W.
The Dead Poet . . . . Shea M.
To a Girl who would like to Stay . . . . Evie F.
The High Line . . . . Leigh V.F.
The Pacific . . . . .Angela S.
Santa Monica Pier . . . . Maggie H.
Eros . . . . Nicholas P.
The Abbey . . . . Ben B., Austin H., Ming Fen C., Maddie P.
A Caged Bird Set Free . . . . V.M.W.
59 Rue de Rivoli. . . . . Caro C.
The Poet of Notre Dame . . . . Mathieu C.R.
Midsummer Muses . . . . My Starlight Poets
Wall of Love . . . . Lies G.
Artist 64 . . . . Béro
Stargazers . . . . My Sunflower Poets
Tavolo 40 . . . . .Mel D. & Denae T.
Edinburgh Cafe, 2022. . . . . .Savannah S.
The Professor. . . . . .Joe G. & Arthur S.
Horoscope for Diana . . . . .Diana M.
St. Dunstan-in-the-East . . . . Bailey R.
Paddington . . . . Carley C.
Hope Speaks to the Hesitant . . . . Ethan G.R.
Artists admiring Artists . . . . Laura C.
Love from Kew. Monica M.
The Floating City . . . . Lauren R.W.
The Secret Library. . . . . .Biddy H.
The Docent . . . . .Kimberly S.

About the Author

Rachel Clift is a poet, artist, & traveler based in the mountains of East Tennessee. More than anything— she longs to inspire people. This is her seventh full collection of poetry— written over the course of two years from 2021 to 2023.

She is a firm believer that traveling with only a backpack and little to no plans is the most marvelous thing one can do and no matter how many times a heart may break— it will always keep beating.

RCLIFTPOETRY.COM @R.CLIFTPOETRY

www.ingramcontent.com/pod-product-compliance
Lightning Source LLC
Chambersburg PA
CBHW020241010526
44107CB00039B/1457/J